Investing For Beginners:

Basic Investment Strategies

By

Robert Alderman

ISBN-13: 978-1495920486

Table of Contents

1. Introduction 5
2. The Fundamentals of Investing Your Money 7
    2.1 Stock Market Investing Fundamentals 8
    2.2 Real Estate Investing Fundamentals 11
    2.3 Precious Metals Investing Fundamentals 15
    2.4 Stock Market Investment Strategy 16
    2.5 Real Estate Investing Strategy 19
    2.6 Precious Metals Investing Strategy 21
    2.7 Options Investing Strategies 22
    2.8 Futures Investing Strategies 27
    2.9 Bond Investing Strategies 32
3. Final Thoughts 37
Thank You Page 38

Investing For Beginners: Basic Investment Strategies

By Robert Alderman

© Copyright 2013 Robert Alderman

Reproduction or translation of any part of this work beyond that permitted by section 107 or 108 of the 1976 United States Copyright Act without permission of the copyright owner is unlawful. Requests for permission or further information should be addressed to the author.

This publication is designed to provide accurate and authoritative information in regard to the subject matter covered. This work is sold with the understanding that the publisher is not engaged in rendering legal, accounting, or other professional services. If legal advice or other expert assistance is required, the services of a competent professional person should be sought.

First Published, 2013

Printed in the United States of America

1. Introduction

As a beginning investor, it's important to know and understand the basic investment strategies that will ultimately help you achieve success in this endeavor.

So many people try to earn money when investing for beginners, but they often overlook the fundamentals and they just don't know how to properly invest so that it becomes a profitable situation.

I'd like to help dispel some of the myths about this topic today. I'd also like to share some insight by teaching you the fundamentals, telling you about some of the best types of investments, and I'd even like to lay out a few investments strategies that you should definitely try.

You see, when investing for beginners, this is often a difficult and daunting task. But I don't want it to be so impossible that you quit before you even begin. That wouldn't help you at all, and it will leave you in a negative situation from a financial standpoint.

Why not allow your money to make more money for you? Isn't that the American dream? Isn't that how our parents and teachers taught us to live?

Basic investment strategies are the key to ultimate success in the world of investing. Plus, it's important that you know as much about investing as you can before you begin. This way you'll avoid any foolish mistakes and begin capitalizing on your investments as soon as possible.

Let's jump into the content of Investing For Beginners: Basic Investment Strategies book...

2. The Fundamentals of Investing Your Money

First, I think it's wise to start out with the fundamentals of stock market investing. Many people invest in the stock market, but they don't always know how to properly diversify. This is usually an area where many people fail. So I wanted to share some of the more specific details with you today.

2.1 Stock Market Investing Fundamentals

To start with, I just want to remind you that there's never a perfect time to invest. As the billionaire investor Warren Buffett often says, you need to be greedy when others are fearful and fearful when others are greedy.

How does this translate into good investment strategies? Well, you have to follow the markets closely and invest in things that you know and understand.

Let's take a look at a quick example…

We've all heard of Coca-Cola, right? We all know that the world loves drinking cola, and it's a craze that isn't going to disappear anytime soon.

Wouldn't this make an excellent investment? I know Warren Buffett thought it would, and it's one of his most successful stock market investments to this very day.

You see, Warren Buffett realized that the love for Coca-Cola was not going to disappear. As a matter of fact, he trusted that of the Coca-Cola Company would expand their brand on a national level. And that's exactly what they did.

So, as Warren Buffett and Berkshire Hathaway bought millions upon millions of shares of this stock, they were able to turn it into billions of dollars over the length of the time of their investment.

It's also a great investment because it pays dividends. Dividends are often paid out quarterly, but in some cases they are even paid on a monthly basis.

When a company has excess capital, they often like to give it back to their investors. The investors receive this money in the form of a dividend. This money goes directly into your trading account, and you could either use it to reinvest in the business by purchasing more shares or you can put the money in your pocket and save it for a rainy day. It's up to you how you decide to use your successful investment earnings.

Diversification is another important concept that you need to learn to grasp. You see, many investors often fail because they put all of their eggs in one basket. Instead of purchasing a smaller amount of shares across multiple companies, they invest everything they have into one company because someone told them that it would be the next big thing.

That is a foolish way to invest, and if you ever want to put all of your money at risk, then that's what you should do. But if you want to safely invest your money and earn good returns, then diversification is the key to making real capital while having your money work for you.

2.2 Real Estate Investing Fundamentals

Okay, so now it's time to touch upon the fundamentals of real estate investing. This is another incredible way to earn money in large chunks or passively. It's up to you which investment strategy makes the most sense. We'll discuss investment strategies a little later in this article, but for now we are going to take a look at the fundamentals.

For starters, if you plan to buy real estate and flip it to earn a lump sum profit, then the fundamentals are very simple. When you invest in real estate, you need to find a property that is selling for less than other comparable properties in the same neighborhood.

Let's take a quick look at an example to help drive this point home…

Say you find a beautiful three bedroom home in South Beach and it's selling for $600,000.

That's an awful lot of money for a single-family, three bedroom apartment.

As a matter of fact, the going rate in the neighborhood is roughly $200,000-$300,000 for a three family home. What makes this property so special? Why is it for sale at such a high price?

Well, there could be a number of reasons why this property is selling at such a high cost. Maybe it's a step above all of the other properties in the neighborhood. Maybe the owner sunk hundreds of thousands of dollars into the home, and completely renovated and revitalized the property.

As an investor looking to flip a property, this is probably not the home for you. Since the going rate in the market is around $200,000-$300,000, you should look for a home that's selling for $100,000-$150,000 or less if you can find it.

You'll probably have to fix the house up in order to get it into selling condition. But you'll be able to turn around and put it on the market for the going rate. If the combination of the purchase price and your expenses are lower than what you sell the property for, then you'll make the difference in one lump sum.

As an example, let's say you purchase a house for $100,000. It's a fixer-upper, and you have to spend about $50,000 in order to get it in selling condition. But once it's fixed up, you put it on the market for $300,000 and sell it for $275,000.

So, you spent $150,000 to make $275,000. That's a profit of $125,000, although it will be less after you pay taxes and brokerage fees. But when looking at gross figures, that's precisely how much you'll make before all of your fees.

As you can see, real estate investing can be quite profitable. But it's not the only investment opportunity out there today. As a matter of fact, I have another excellent option that I'm going to share with you now.

2.3 Precious Metals Investing Fundamentals

Precious metals are an excellent area to invest and many people do not realize it.

If you check the historical charts for gold and silver dating back to 2001, you'll see that both commodities rose about 600% from that point until 2011.

Since then, precious metals have been pulling back in price. This is not a bad thing at all, because the economy is in shambles and the US dollar is not doing so well. As an investor in precious metals, you get to hedge your bets against inflation which is directly tied into the US dollar, and you also get to avoid the worries of investing during a troubled economy.

Even though the price of gold and silver has dropped, the bull market has not come to an end. As a matter of fact, the drop in price has created an excellent buying opportunity for those interested in capitalizing on this market. If you missed the big rise in price between 2001 and 2011, you now have a chance to buy precious metals cheaply and make an excellent return all at the same time.

I don't know about you, but the opportunity with precious metals is a favored investment strategy of mine. It's the one commodity that never goes out of fashion. Gold and silver have been used as forms of currency since the beginning of recorded history. That's never going to change, and it's only going to become more prevalent as banks continue to fail and the US dollar continues to falter.

Let's now take a look at some of the ways to strategically invest in all three of these areas. We'll begin with an investment strategy that's perfect for those looking to trade stocks...

2.4 Stock Market Investment Strategy

I already touched upon this, but it bears repeating. Diversification is king when investing in the stock market. Otherwise you leave yourself vulnerable to the ups and downs that a single stock will often go through during in the cyclical trends in the marketplace.

As an investor, if you only plan to invest in one company that you feel strongly about, then you need to follow the trends of that industry. There will be certain times when that stock falls out of favor. There's nothing you can do about this. It won't negatively affect you as long as you follow the trends and understand how the market works.

But here's the thing...

Most people do not have the financial knowledge or time to follow the market so closely. It's a much safer bet to diversify your investments and invest in a multitude of companies that you feel strongly about.

Maybe you like a specific company in the food services industry. You should certainly purchase shares if you feel strongly about the investment. Or maybe you like a company in the oil and natural gas industry. That's another company to add to your investment portfolio.

I recommend that you look through the various sectors on the stock market, and pick the company most likely to succeed in that sector. If you do this across a multitude of sectors, you will not fall victim to the ups and downs in the marketplace since your money will be spread out and the risk will be absorbed through diversification.

Let's see what else we have in store...

2.5 Real Estate Investing Strategy

If you plan to invest in real estate for passive income, here's an excellent strategy that you that you might want to follow.

When you buy a property, make sure the mortgage is low enough that your monthly rent roll will be able to cover the mortgage and put money in your pocket.

Here's an example to help see what I mean…

You buy a three family home for $500,000. Luckily, you have a decent amount for a down payment so you immediately pay off half of the home. Now you only have a $250,000 mortgage to pay over a period of 30 years.

You'll be living in one of the apartments and renting out the other two. So, let's say your monthly mortgage is $2000. If you'd like to pay off the mortgage each month through the rent roll, and put $500 in your pocket as well, then you'll need to rent each apartment for $1250.

That's the strategy and it's very effective at paying off your property and earning a passive income.

2.6 Precious Metals Investing Strategy

This strategy is very simple. If you believe that the US and world economy is going to continue to struggle for some time, then you should start putting your money in precious metals.

You see, as these economies struggle and their currencies falter, the value of precious metals will continue to rise. That's the strategy in a nutshell and it's very simple to implement.

2.7 Options Investing Strategies

Option investing is described as a privilege sold by one investor to another; this privilege allows the buyer the right to buy or to sell a security at a price as well as the time or date that has been agreed upon by the two parties. There are two types of options: a call is a privilege of the holder of the stock to dictate the right price, time and date. Buyers anticipate that the stock will increase before the option expires. A put on the other hand is the privilege of the holder of the stock to sell at a specific price in a specified period of time. Buyers anticipate that the price of the stock is higher than the current market value to be able to easily gain huge profits.

Investors that would like to try options investments should have a high risk tolerance since most stock prices may fluctuate from 30-40% in a 24 hour time frame. If you use options in the most efficient way it can become a tool in hedging against a position in the market.

The type of options trading strategy that you may use may depend on what kind of options trader you are.

Speculator

As the name suggests, speculators buy an option based on their belief on how the stock will behave within a particular span of time. Speculation may be due to a variety of factors but this is an all-or-nothing strategy so be prepared to either get the most out of your investments or lose everything you got.

Hedging

In placing a hedge in your stock investment, you specify how much you are planning to sell your stock in a specified date and time which clearly reduces any risks. You may buy stocks or bonds and hold on to your investments for a while (for months to years) and then sell them when you think the time is right. You hedge the risk and you maintain a firm grasp on your investments instead of using speculations in your investment strategy.

Other options strategies

Options are similar to stocks and are purchased from a discount or a full-service broker. To be able to start trading options you will have to be approved first and this is done through a brokerage firm. Your knowledge of how the market works will be assessed as well as you experience before you will get an approval. Options are purchased through creating a margin account or a borrowed money account.

Depending on how you would like to use your hard earned cash you should never rely on foolish notions when dealing with options or stocks investments. The best strategy that you should employ is using the services of a stock broker or a brokerage firm. By using the services of a professional, you will be rest assured that you will be able to get the best out of your investments through the use of sound financial and investment practices and the use of tools to help you weed out unnecessary theories in investment.

Options are one of the most difficult types of investments to deal with being a beginner in options investments is no joke. By letting an experienced broker guide you, your investments will be protected and you will even learn how to deal with options investing on your own.

Watchful waiting

Options are also considered highly complex and anyone interested in investing in options should watch and wait for the market. Having a close eye on your investment means you should be aware of the factors that can influence the price of your stocks in the market as well as the potential movements of other stocks that may also affect your investment. You must also learn to be patient and have a high tolerance for risk and stress since there is sometimes a huge movement in the market that can leverage your investments. You should also strive to equip yourself with the latest information about the market and not just carry the basics of investing.

2.8 Futures Investing Strategies

Futures is the term used to denote investments on various commodities, stock market indexes, and currencies in an attempt to predict the value of these investments in the future or at a particular date in the future. Financial advisers mostly caution investors against their interest in investing in futures since it carries a very high amount of risk. Although this recommendation may be true, futures investment may just be the same as investing in bonds and stocks. Futures may also be used by investors to hedge against risk. And to counter the risks involved in investing futures, there are strategies that an investor may use to ensure that he protects his return of investment.

Hedging

Hedging is one of the most popular ways to remove or reduce the risk of a futures investment. For instance you a own a stock and then you sold a futures contract that states you will sell your stock at a set price which eliminates the threat of fluctuations and changes in the market price. Oftentimes hedging is used even by the most experienced investors especially when they are unsure of the current market.

There are types of hedging. One type is the perfect hedge where any potential risk is eliminated. Most say that it is impossible to create a perfect hedge and most are either classified as imperfect or near-perfect hedges.

A protective put hedge is a type of hedge wherein a holder of a security uses a put to guard his investments against a drop in the price. This is used when a trader is bullish on the investment stocks that he already owns but is uncertain of the market. Investors and analysts agree that there is no limit to the profit that may be attained with the use of a put hedge.

A trader that deals with futures can use a hedge to protect this futures position from a synthetic futures position. Business owners use this strategy especially when the business uses or produces raw materials; owners can reduce the potential risk on the price of commodities by hedging through a community futures market. Future purchase price of a particular commodity may be locked using long hedge strategies while the selling price of a commodity may be locked using a short hedge.

A spread

Or futures spread is also known as an arbitrage technique. This is when a trader or investor purchases a commodity and sells a contract of the same type of commodity to capitalize in any changes or differences in prices. The ultimate goal in using futures spread is to earn from the change in the prices between two futures and all the while hedging against any risk that may affect your investment.

Futures spread trading is considered profitable and at the same time easy to trade. There is less risk compared to using straight futures, there is lower margins needed, the trades are less volatile and trends are steeper and are for a longer period of time.

Speculating

Speculating is a form of futures investment that aims to profit by betting on the direction on where the asset is moving or headed to. It is the job of speculators to make a smart guess on where the market will be at a given time and he will base his activity on his speculations. For instance, if a speculator believes that a stock is overpriced he may short sell an wait when the prices will decline. Upon this speculation, he will then wait for the right time to purchase back the stock and get the profits that he has been speculating on. This is a risky futures investment strategy and is prone to being affected by the downside and possible upside of the market but maximum profits are possible when speculations gain positive results.

2.9 Bond Investing Strategies

Bond investing is simply buying bonds with the maximum amount of yield. Investors and financial advisers say that beginners that are interested in bond investing should create a bond portfolio. But finding a lucrative certificate of deposit for a bond is not as easy as it looks; you may employ several strategies that may help you get a maximum return of your investment.

Passive bond

In a passive bond strategy, the buy and hold of buying bonds is all about holding bonds until their value matures. Since this is a passive strategy, there are no assumptions made on the future of the interest rate and any factors that may influence the value of the bond is not important to the investor. It is as simple as purchasing the bond in a premium price and receiving the full value upon maturity. Passive bond investment may seem to be perceived as a lazy-style of bond investment but it actually grounds the investors from suffering from financial troubles.

Bond laddering

This is a form of passive bond investing where in the investor's portfolio is divided into parts in a laddered style. A ladder clearly shows how an investment is predicted to be worth over a certain period of time. By using a laddered strategy, an investor will be able to maximize strategies that can help him receive a steady equal cash flow annually.

Indexing bond

This is a semi-passive bond investment strategy that aims to get a huge return while the risks are minimized comparable to a targeted index strategy. But even when it is has some characteristics of a buy and hold passive bond strategy it may also be flexible in the sense that it can be structured to look like a published bond index such as the Lehman

Aggregate Bond Index. This is a great technique if you plan to build a large portfolio; several factors should be included such as periodic assessment and rebalancing of the entries to reflect accurate changes in the price of your bonds.

Immunization bond

This is a strategy that protects an investment portfolio for a specific period of time regardless of any factors that can influence its interest rates. Comparable to buy and hold strategies, an immunization bond strategy is best suited for high-grade bonds. Pure immunization bond strategies may be applied to investing in zero-coupon bonds; this matches the maturity of the bond to the date of which the cash flow is expected.

The duration or what investors call the average life of a bond is often seen in immunization bond strategies. It is a predictive measure of the volatility of a bond and is used in large scale investments. Considering the duration of the bond is a very sound strategy since it does not just work for large businesses but will also work for individuals that would like to create his own investment portfolio or simply a plan intended for his retirement.

Active bond

An active investment strategy is the very opposite of passive investing since you use all the tools and strategies you can to have a maximum return of investment. There are some risks involved but studying the market closely could minimize these. There are styles used in active bond investment like timing, valuation, entertaining interest rate scenarios, interest rate anticipation, spread exploitation and so many more. An active strategy is basically about the investor's willingness to bet on the future of his investments rather than rely on passive strategies.

Additional strategies

A brokerage firm or a stock broker will help you manage your investments in the most beneficial way. Bond investment may look easy but beginners should consider sound and well-practiced strategies from experienced professionals. Not only will you be getting a return of your investment but you will also learn how to invest using your own skills and knowledge of the market. When you already know the basics of bond investment and have mastered confidence in trading on your own then you will soon be able to make your own decisions when it comes to investing in bonds.

3. Final Thoughts

As a beginner, I know investing your money can be very scary. But you have to invest if you're going to retire comfortably in this day and age. At this point, investing is a must. So recognize the value in investing, and implement some of the strategies mentioned above. You'll be on the road to investing success in no time at all.

Thank You Page

I want to personally thank you for reading my book. I hope you found information in this book useful and I would be very grateful if you could leave your honest review about this book. I certainly want to thank you in advance for doing this.

www.ingramcontent.com/pod-product-compliance
Lightning Source LLC
Chambersburg PA
CBHW070723180526

45167CB00004B/1596